T0258198

## Hometown Honorees

Blackstone Mayor Billy Coleburn presented 'Black History Heroes' plaques Saturday during the Town's Juneteenth Celebration. LEFT PHOTO: Shirley Austin Smith (accepting on behalf of honoree Rev. Dr. Frank Tucker); honoree Barbara Thompson; and Celeste Wynn, daughter of honoree the late Constance Wynn. RIGHT PHOTO: honoree Christine Davis Easterling, who offered brief remarks about her time at the former Luther Foster High School. As she has done since 2019, she continued her call for Nottoway officials to rename the old high school in Dr. Foster's memory.

Black History Heroes, Class of 2022

**BLACKSTONE JUNETEENTH**

June 25, 2022

FOREWORD BY **MAYOR WILLIAM D. (BILLY) COLEBURN**
BLACKSTONE, VIRGINIA

# *Juneteenth*

## THE **REAL TRUTH** AND
## HOW IT BEGAN IN MY HOMETOWN

## *Christine Easterling*

**By the Same Author:**

*Inspirational Treasures: Essays by Educators and the Students Reflecting the Joys of Teaching*

*A Giant for Justice: Inspirational Biography of William H. "Bill" Simons III*

*Divine \*Miraculous\* Magnificent: The Miracles of Jesus*

*You Can Move Your Mountains: Keep Pushing with Your Mountain-Moving Faith*

*Methods of Teaching Children in the Home: Parents and Children Facing Unprecedented Times at Home*

© BookBaby
Independent Publishing Platform
7905 N. Crescent Blvd., Pennsauken, NJ 08110

# CONTENTS

# MAYOR WILLIAM D. (BILLY) COLEBURN

*Christine Davis Easterling is a positive force. She is intelligent and inquisitive and just as compassionate and caring as she is tenacious.*

*When she gets a thought in her head or mission on her mind, there's no stopping her. She's as sharp, quick-witted, and energetic as people half her age.*

*I've known her for only a few years, yet I feel as if I've known her my whole my life. I call her "teacher" not only because she's a retired, successful, career educator, but she continues to teach me and show me new perspectives. She also gives me 'assignments' from time to time, and she sees to it that I complete them! Did I mention that she's quite persuasive?*

*While there is no one else on earth like Christine Easterling, her childhood experiences mirror those of many others who grew-up in segregated Blackstone.*

*She lived within sight of a majestic campus—Blackstone College for Girls—a place she knew that she and others who looked like her would never be welcomed or allowed to attend.*

*Christine Davis Easterling is another proud, successful product of old Luther H. Foster High School (1950–70). What that institution may have lacked in funding and resources was more than offset by faculty and staff's love, dedication, and emphasis on self-discipline. That all-Black school in Nottoway County produced doctors, attorneys, engineers, warriors, educators, nurses, career civil servants, and many others who contributed greatly to the America we love today.*

*I am honored to be featured in Mrs. Easterling's work. On paper, I'd be one of the last people to be invited to write a foreword for a book on Juneteenth and race relations.*

*I grew-up a privileged Southern white boy and went to a private school that didn't admit Black students until the late 1980s. My parents gave me everything I ever needed, yet they also instilled in me the values of courtesy and decency toward all others.*

*My mother was adored by many in the Black community—not only for her warmth, kindness, and Southern hospitality. Her brothers, the late Dr. Epes Harris and the late Dr. James Harris, gave Blacks the same medical care, dignity, and compassion as they did whites. That included house calls and delivering babies in the middle of the night.*

*It wasn't until I returned home in 1990 from The College of William & Mary that it hit me—there were two very different Blackstones. Privilege had given me the false impression that all was well in our little town. It was, but only for some of us.*

*And it wasn't until I ran for Mayor at age thirty-seven that I realized not only was it okay here to talk about race, there was a longing, a yearning to discuss it and embrace our differences and that yes, there is much we have in common—economic challenges, worries about our children, and love of God.*

*Both my Uncle James (who served as Mayor from 1982-2006), and my father, who in his younger years was a champion of segregation as was his father, told me that Black people appreciate sincere communication and effort, and they also know a con artist when they see one. That's because for too long, Blacks weren't appreciated and in fact were ignored, and for too long they were lied to, especially by white politicians.*

*I grew up watching my father get on his knees every night at the foot of his bed praying to God with both hands together, his elbows resting on the mattress. While he's far from perfect on race relations—as are so many of us—he once told me that he shouldn't say such a thing but he believed Blacks generally have a deeper and more personal faith in God.*

*I asked him why. "Because, son," he told me as we rode around the countryside, "look at how they've been treated since their arrival in this country and look at how devoutly they worship."*

*It took me serving as Mayor to learn more about my town and its racial complexities. We have made much progress as a WHOLE community, investing in low-income neighborhoods and preserving that tax base so that Blackstone today can offer a wide array of services to all.*

*While celebrating Juneteenth does not rid Blackstone of its unpleasant and unfair past—no celebration can do that—it does remind us of how far we've come, and the greater things possible in the future if we continue to work hand in hand and walk forward together. There was a time in my life when many would cringe or feel uncomfortable celebrating the freedom of slaves because doing so required one to remember that our people held other people in bondage for hundreds of years. Life is too short to cringe. Let us celebrate today and cherish the advances we have made, as well as the grace, strength, and perseverance of Christine Davis Easterling and so many others.*

**-Mayor William D (Billy) Coleburn**

Mayor William Billy Coleburn is the retired mayor of Blackstone, Virginia. He is also the publisher of the Blackstone Courier Newspaper. He is editor of the Courier-Record in Blackstone and in his fourteenth year as mayor of his hometown.

He has been at the paper since 1990 and is the third-generation Coleburn to run it. His family acquired the paper in 1946, and his ninety-six-year-old father, Doug, still writes a column or two every week. He's been at the paper since June 1948.

Billy is a fifty-five-year-old worry-a-holic and work-a-holic who takes out his frustrations by running, working out, and meditating. He enjoys Corona Light with limes and loves sports and debating (civilly) and politics and learning from one another. Transparency is a BIG DEAL for him because he has covered and served with quite a few people who don't believe in it, and in fact, loathe it but don't mind using the t-word when politicking. He loves his family and his town and his state and his country. He likes to laugh (loves comedy, Jim Carey, Robin Williams, etc.) and loves to compete, especially on the golf course. Despite being an introvert, he enjoys talking to lots of different people. It exhausts him, but he enjoys it; He just has to crash afterward and recharge. Then he does it all over again. He enjoys being alone. He will often sit outside by himself after work, for hours, just looking and reflecting.

"He's a local official and knows what it's like to have to answer questions," she says. "He believes in giving the public as much information as you possibly can. Billy gives out everything that's required and often is looking for ways to give out further information. It's a real breath of fresh air for the FOIA council."

If Blackstone is a small pond, then Billy Coleburn '90, is a big fish as both mayor of the 3,600-person Southside Virginia town and editor of the independently owned Courier-Record newspaper. He presides over Town Council meetings and reports on government actions. He throws the ceremonial first pitch at little league games and covers the crowning of the prom king and queen.

After growing up in a racially segregated environment, William & Mary exposed him to a diverse student population. As a political science and government major, he learned about the history of the Voting Rights Act, the dangers of the executive branch holding too much power, and the importance of transparency and accountability in government—lessons that would guide him both as a journalist and as an elected official.

Living and working in close proximity to readers promotes accountability, he says: "I see the people at Food Lion, the post office, and at church. I think that aspect makes him a fairer journalist."

The Coleburns have two daughters, Caroline, who followed her father and grandfather's footsteps into journalism and works as a television news reporter in Richmond, Virginia, and Mary Katherine, who attended William & Mary.

Journalists and public officials sometimes find themselves at odds given the traditional "watchdog" role of newspapers, but Billy Coleburn says the key to navigating the dual roles is fairness and transparency.

That's especially important in a locality that's almost evenly divided between Blacks and whites, Democrats and Republicans. Coleburn, who is conservative politically, won reelection as mayor in 2018 with seventy-two percent of the vote against a Democratic-leaning opponent.

Billy grew up attending an all-white private school and playing baseball in a segregated little league, but as mayor and newspaper editor, he strives to ensure that everyone's voice can be heard.

Lewis "Peanut" Johnson, a community advocate who has occasionally, bumped heads with Coleburn, says that after he expressed concerns about the need for more recognition of African American residents, the mayor initiated a Black History Heroes program during the month of February to highlight Blackstone natives who achieved success despite the racial barriers they confronted. Coleburn also supported a proposal from Johnson and other Black residents for a March Against Racism in 2019. The mayor participated in the event and encouraged Johnson to keep attending meetings and speaking up.

Coleburn says he first decided to run for mayor of Blackstone in 2006, after sixteen years of covering meetings for local governing bodies, because of frustration with how unresponsive he felt elected officials were when residents voiced concerns at meetings.

"There was very little dialogue between elected officials and those they serve," he says. "As mayor, I love a packed house because everyone's watching. A government that is watched governs best."

"Billy plays an important role in providing government transparency and protecting a free press," says Betsy Edwards, executive director of the Virginia Press Association. Coleburn also served on the association's board from 2016-20.

"Many of the issues related to the Freedom of Information Act involve local government, and as the only member who is both an elected official and a journalist, Coleburn can see things from both sides," Edwards says. When local government officials on the council make excuses for why they can't provide information, he challenges them.

# DEDICATION

I dedicate this book to my mother, Harriet Ann Davis, and my father, Lynwood Davis Jr. who were lifetime residents of Blackstone. They will not be forgotten, and I thank them for naming me after Jesus Christ. The name Christine means follower of Christ.

I further write this dedication to all Blackstone residents and other cities, towns, and states throughout our country, making it all possible for me to write this book about Juneteenth in my Hometown, Blackstone, Virginia.

I further dedicate this book to, William D. (Billy) Coleburn the Mayor of Blackstone, Virginia in Nottoway County who has supported me throughout the years in my efforts to eradicate systematic racism in Nottoway County. I appreciate him for his deep and abiding commitment to justice and equality.

When the Mayor of Blackstone, Virginia decided to institute a Juneteenth Festival in 2021 and another in 2022, I felt that he was joining the struggle to educate and elevate citizens about Juneteenth.

His efforts as a fifty-four-year-old mayor motivated me to write this book about the two Juneteenth festivals he has held in my small, segregated town of Blackstone, which includes about 4,000 residents. I want to applaud my hometown residents who worked diligently to make sure that they taught the meaning of Juneteenth and celebrated it appropriately. Many of us did not know the meaning of Juneteenth and had not ever celebrated it.

My book will show appreciation to my hometown for its festivals and telling the truth about Juneteenth.

After the two major celebrations in my hometown, my major research about Juneteenth began to reach new altitudes.

I was driven to continue to participate in celebrations and further educate the world by writing a book about Juneteenth in my hometown.

# PREFACE

I wrote this book about Juneteenth because I have always been an advocate for justice and reparation in my hometown and throughout the nation.

In this book, I present the truth about Juneteenth with reference to Juneteenth in my hometown, about the efforts Blackstone put forth, to see that Juneteenth is taught and that people learn and celebrate it.

Mayor William (Billy) D. Coleburn has supported me through his Blackstone Courier Newspaper for over two years in my efforts to fight the Nottoway County School Board for reparations regarding discrimination of a Black College President by not putting his name on a Black School in Nottoway County. He knew that I would not give up because I also believe that one will never see the end if we give up in the middle.

When the mayor also decided to institute a Juneteenth Festival in 2021 and another in 2022, I felt that he was not going to give hate a safe harbor.

His efforts as a young 54-year-old Mayor motivated me to write this book about the two Juneteenth festivals that he held in my small racist town of Blackstone which includes about 4,000 residents. I want to applaud my hometown residents who worked diligently to make sure that they taught the meaning of Juneteenth and celebrated it appropriately.

Many of us did not know the meaning of Juneteenth and had not ever celebrated it.

My book will show appreciation to my hometown for its festivals and tell the truth about Juneteenth. It was said that Juneteenth is built on falsehoods and wrapped in mistruths. After this major celebration in my hometown, my major research about Juneteenth began to reach new heights. I was driven to continue contributing to Juneteenth, participating in celebrations, and further educating the world by writing a book about Juneteenth.

I wrote a special letter to Mayor Coleburn which he published in The Blackstone Courier Newspaper.

I appreciate The Town of Blackstone for producing its first and second Annual Black History Heroes Program. I congratulate Mayor Coleburn for his efforts to recognize native sons and daughters and long-time residents—past and present—who overcame obstacles and achieved success in industry, business, medicine, law, education, public service, and community involvement. I ask that he continue to seize the opportunity to honor the too often neglected accomplishments of Black Americans in every area of endeavor in the town of Blackstone. This program will promote a growing awareness of Black identity and achievements by Black Americans and other people of African descent.

Additionally, I express my gratitude for receiving one of the mayor's Black History Hero Awards for 2021. I am more than honored to have received it at the First Annual Juneteenth Celebration.

# ACKNOWLEDGEMENTS

This book goes forth with heartfelt prayer and hopes that God, the Lord of the harvest, will be pleased with the use of this book as a teaching instrument for the Black History Education of youth and adults around the world.

I would like to express my gratitude to the support system that has been the source of numerous thoughts and illustrations in this book.

I am therefore thankful and I acknowledge my indebtedness and appreciation to my Photographer, Paul Jones, Black History Hero Warren Johnson, the Mayor of Blackstone, Virginia who wrote the foreword, my cousins Sharon Clark Taylor and Warren Johnson Jr., my sorority sisters, Earlene Evans, Teola Jones and Pamela Benson, Deaconess Emma Smith, Pastors Rev. Glen Benson and Rev. Frank D. Tucker, Trustee Samuel McCoy, and Black History Hero William Clark.

I give heartfelt thanks to Committee members Chastity Bryant and Arlene Robinson for their messages, motivation, and endless support.

I am eternally grateful to my photographer Paul Jones who recorded the entire Juneteenth event.

# INTRODUCTION

Blackstone's 2022 Juneteenth celebration was held on Saturday, June 25th, from 10 a.m. to 10 p.m. in the Historic Business District downtown.

The committee planned events that included a vendor welcome/ kick-off in Crewe on Friday evening, June 24th, and countywide worship Sunday morning, and other events were on June 26th, at the Nottoway Middle School Auditorium.

*Shelia Jones, Chandra Lewis, William Clarke, Danielle Pinto, Nick, Kim Robertson, Arlene Robertson, Annette Felder, Lewis Johnson, Chastiddy Bryant, Janet Wilson, Ellen Eppes, Shirverne Griffin, Erielle Eppes, Nathanial Miller, Clarence Hawkes*

# TOWN OF BLACKSTONE JUNETEENTH CELEBRATION 2021, 2022

By: Caroline Coleburn, WTVR Chanel 6 News

Richmond, Virginia

Posted at 11:00 AM, Jun 21, 2022

BLACKSTONE, Va.—The small town of Blackstone will hold its second annual Juneteenth on the 25, 2022.

The multi-day event kicks off Friday evening, but the big events will be held on Saturday starting at 10 a.m. in the Historic Business District downtown.

There will be vendors, educational speakers, live music, a place for children, and county-wide worship on Sunday at the Nottoway Middle School Auditorium.

Virginia State University President Dr. Makola Abdullah will give the keynote address at the event.

The small town of 3,500 had more than 3,000 people show up last year, and they expect an even larger crowd this year.

# JUNETEENTH CELEBRATION IN BLACKSTONE

## Chastiddy Bryant, Director of Community Development

First, I want to say Thank you, Lord, for allowing the Nottoway County Juneteenth Celebration to have so much success. Without you, none of this would be possible.

Second, I would like to thank the ENTIRE Juneteenth Committee for working together to pull off a weekend to remember. Third, I would like to thank all vendors, performers, speakers, and participants. Thank you for participating, and being patient as we worked to give you an event where you could shine. Without their knowledge and wisdom, our history and futures would be without worth.

To all volunteers, your selfless acts of kindness touched all of our lives this weekend.

To 101.1 The Fam, your team has been amazing to work with and we hope for continued success for your station and for your involvement next year.

To all the local businesses that participated, you are the reason we can make this county a united blessing for others to see. It shows that unity lives in the heart of Blackstone VA, and no matter how small we may be, we can inspire small towns all over the world to celebrate independence for all. Not just the Fourth of July but Juneteenth as well.

We don't want division, just inclusion and equality for all, and by participating, we see that you are the backbone of our celebration.

For those who chose not to participate, we respect your decision and hopefully, next year you will.

For all officers, your efforts made this event safe for all attendees. You help make the committee's job easier and we thank you for all your help and service.

For the towns of Crewe, Burkeville, Blackstone, and Nottoway County for your sponsorships, dedication, and support, we will forever be grateful.

To the Town of Blackstone workers who worked long hours and kept the event beautiful the entire day. You guys do the job that doesn't get the most recognition but deserves an abundance of appreciation, and without hesitation fix anything at the drop of a hat. I salute you all!

To the churches who assisted all weekend long. God sent us true angels and we were beyond blessed with your help, support, guidance, and words.

Last but not least, to ALL ATTENDEES. You all are our inspiration. We aspire to educate others and hope children learn as they enjoy the events, activities, and shows. If you have photos, please share them. As many members could not enjoy all parts, we would love to see your smiles at the annual Juneteenth Celebration. Please tag us Annual Juneteenth Celebration – See everyone next year for bigger and better!!!

# REMEMBER PLANT A SEED!

## Arlene Robertson, History Sub-Committee

Good morning family and friends,

Saturday, June 25th marks the second town of Blackstone Juneteenth celebration. We have worked as hard this year as we did last year to present a Juneteenth celebration that we hope each of you will enjoy and learn something that you did not know regarding the celebration.

My place on the committee is working with the history sub-committee. Our committee will feature speakers and presenters in the New Life Church beginning at 10:00 a.m. The speakers that I personally invited are:

10:00: Reverend Damion T. Batts, Pastor of Mount Nebo Baptist Church, who will be speaking on, "The Role of the Church in the African American Community."

11:00: Ms. Thelma Austin, Washington, DC, Author of *My Family Voices*, will be speaking on "Legacy of the Black Family in the Community."

12:00: Mrs. Shirley Lee, Author/Educator Lunenburg County: Speaking on "Education in the Black Community Pre-integration."

2:00: Mrs. Paula Bonds, Music Education/Virginia Symphony Orchestra, Norfolk, VA. Mrs. Bonds will be speaking/presenting on genealogy. This has become a subject of great interest to many of us in the past twenty years. Paula is a former Band Director of Nottoway High School.

Other speakers for the day in New Life Church include:

11:45: Mr. Rodney Reynolds the First Black General Registrar for Nottoway County: "Voting in the African American community.

1:00: Ms. Brenda White: Domestic Violence

3:00: Ms. Lataisia Jones: African Americans in STEM research as it pertains to biochemistry.

4:00: Mr. Darnell Dixon: African Americans in STEM research as it pertains to NASA.

5:00: Mrs. Patricia Miller Williams, former Nottoway County resident will be speaking on: African American Women in Pageantry.

Your Juneteenth Committee has put forth much time and effort making contacts with vendors, speakers/presenters, and those who are there for your entertainment. I am inviting each of you to New Life Church to hear the information the presenters are bringing to you.

Some of our speakers have had to go through many hardships in life and are willing to share some of their histories with you.

These are they who have blazed trails that our great-grandchildren won't have to endure.

Hope to see each of you on Saturday morning, love you and God's blessings.

# A GREAT DAY IN BLACKSTONE

Dear Mayor Coleburn,

I recognize the town of Blackstone for creating its First Annual Black History Heroes Program. I congratulate you for your efforts to recognize native sons and daughters and longtime residents—past and present—who overcame obstacles and achieved success in industry, business, medicine, law, education, public service, and community involvement.

Continue to seize the opportunity to honor the too often neglected accomplishments of Black Americans in every area of endeavor in the town of Blackstone. Your program will promote a growing awareness of Black identity achievements by Black Americans and other peoples of African descent.

The story of Black History Month began in 1915, half a century after the Thirteenth Amendment abolished slavery in the United States, and you still see the need to acknowledge it. May God continue to bless you for doing his work.

Additionally, I express my gratitude for receiving one of the mayor's Black History Hero Awards for 2021. I am more than honored to have received it at the First Annual Juneteenth Celebration.

Christine Davis Easterling

Author

**William H. Clark**—It was such an honor to receive the Blackstone Black History Hero award on Saturday at Blackstone Virginia Juneteenth Celebration, in Blackstone Virginia. Also receiving the Hero awards were Mrs. Alice Birckhead, Mr. Warren Johnson. and Mr. James L Clarke, my brother. It was such an honor to be on stage with my older brother.

## Warren Johnson – Blackstone Black History Hero Award Recipient

To The Town of Blackstone: The Honorable Mayor Coleburn and members of the Town Council.

I would like to thank you for honoring me with a "Special Recognition Award" as part of the Blackstone Black History Hero Program.

My family roots were planted in the soil of Blackstone in 1829, when my great-grandfather migrated from Amelia County, Virginia. I was raised by a family tradition, to always treat people the way you want to be treated.

The window of my soul reflects Blackstone, and when you do things from your soul, you feel joy. During the festivities this past Saturday, I felt love in the air and joy beneath my feet as I walked the streets of Blackstone. I am proud of my heritage and proud to call Blackstone my hometown.

Again, many thanks to the leadership of the town of Blackstone, my former teachers and classmates from Luther H. Foster High School, and my family.

Warren Johnson, Jr.
—Class of 1962 Luther H. Foster High School

**Earlene Evans – Richmond, Virginia,** I think it is wonderful that you are writing a book about Juneteenth. It should certainly shed light on unfamiliar topics for many.

**Warren Johnson – Accokeek, Maryland.**

**Writing a book about Juneteenth!** WOW! What a great idea! You are always thinking ahead and creating learning resources for future generations to be informed and involved. Clearly, you are a National Treasure.

**Sharon Clark Taylor –**

**So few people knew about Juneteenth.**—It wasn't something that was taught to us in school. I don't know if my parents were aware. They never shared that information with me if they knew. I was full-grown when I learned of events a few years ago. I'm just finding out about Juneteenth in the last few years, I don't know what Information I could provide that you don't already know! But as usual, I'm here.

**Samuel McCoy –**

**So few people knew about Juneteenth.** There was no internet or telephones then to spread the news, so when Union Major Gen. Gordon Granger arrived in Galveston, Texas the most remote outpost of the Southern slave states—on June 19, 1865, there were only unconfirmed rumors about the Emancipation Proclamation that had freed enslaved peoples more than two years earlier, Stevenson said.

# CHAPTER 1

# BLACKSTONE, VIRGINIA— MY HOMETOWN

I am a native of Blackstone, Virginia. Blackstone is a small town in Nottoway County, Virginia. Before the Revolutionary War, it was founded as the settlement of "Blacks and Whites," after two tavern keepers.

When I lived there, it was a segregated town with segregated schools. My county government was so racist that the county refused to put a Black College President's name on the school because he was black.

In the 1850s, it was a stop on the Southside Railroad—the current Norfolk Southern Railway. The grid street pattern for the town was laid out in 1874. On May 11, 1875, it was renamed Bellefonte. However, the name was reverted back to Blacks and Whites in 1882. On February 23, 1886, the town of Blackstone was incorporated after the English jurist William Blackstone. Its economy thrived as a center for dark-leaf tobacco sales and shipment. Today, Blackstone has a total area of 4.6 square miles.

As of the 2000 census, Blackstone had a population of 3,675 people and a population density of 811.8 people per square mile. It is spread out with its racial makeup being 50.23% white, 46.39% African American, 2.39% Hispanic or Latino, 1.88% other races, 9.76% two or more races, 0.71% Asian, and 0.03% Native American

The average income for a household in Blackstone was $27,566. Males make a median income of $26,419, and females make $17,905. The town's per capita was $15,562. In 2000, 26.5% of the population lived below the poverty line. Notable people who have lived in Blackstone are actress Bea Arthur, Bishop James Cannon Jr., U.S. Army soldier Booker T. Spicely, Representative and lawyer James F. Epes, and American football player Robert Jones.

I am now proud of the racial progress my small hometown has made. Celebrating Juneteenth for the first time was a step toward promoting justice and equality. I started doing more and more research on Juneteenth and planned to be there at the second Juneteenth historic celebration. I was in the middle of trying to get the county to do reparation for putting the name Luther H. Foster on a Black school after the county denied the family and the members of the Alumni Association the opportunity to rightfully name the school.

The celebration of Juneteenth in Blackstone represented the emancipation of enslaved people in this country. In 2021, Juneteenth was celebrated as a holiday for the first time. Juneteenth marked the day when, in 1865, enslaved people in Galveston, Texas, discovered they were finally free from being mere property. This took place more than two years after President Abraham Lincoln signed the Emancipation Proclamation.

Juneteenth today not only represents freedom; it also serves as a reminder of the nation's complicated history with race and racism.

The first Juneteenth, in 1866, was commemorated by newly freed Black people taking pride in their status and the event was reportedly marked with communal meals, singing, and church services. And Juneteenth 2022 celebrations will be celebrated worldwide, with the theme recognizing emancipation of all kinds.

# CHAPTER 2

# WHY DIDN'T PEOPLE IN MY HOMETOWN KNOW ABOUT JUNETEENTH?

Juneteenth, which combines the words June and nineteenth, is an *unofficial* national holiday marking the day Major General Gordon Granger of the Union Army read federal orders in the city of Galveston, Texas on June 19th, 1865. The proclamation stated that all slaves in Texas were now free. Readers who know their history also know that this official proclamation came two and a half years after President Lincoln's Emancipation Proclamation, which became official on January 1st, 1863.

African Americans began celebrating Juneteenth within one year of the Galveston Proclamation. According to a PBS article written by scholar-historian Henry Louis Gates, Jr., "In one of the most inspiring grassroots efforts of the post-Civil War period, they [freed slaves] transformed June 19th from a day of unheeded military orders into their own annual rite."

Juneteenth is acknowledged by forty-seven states and the District of Columbia, but it is not a federal holiday. Many African Americans participate in Juneteenth celebrations, which include parades, rodeos, street fairs, family reunions, park parties, cookouts, and music festivals.

Hearon explained the importance of the Juneteenth celebrations, "Growing up in Denver, Juneteenth in Five Points was the highlight of each summer because that's when the Black community would come together to celebrate our emancipation with a street fair, good food, live entertainment, and a parade," she said. "I looked forward to participating."

The holiday does not mark one day but rather, it honors a process of racial equality that is still ongoing. Admissions Counselor Deneshia Hearon, chair of CU Denver's Black Faculty & Staff Affinity Group (BFSA), said, "Juneteenth is not just the end of slavery, but the acknowledgment of freedom." CU Denver Vice Chancellor for Diversity, Equity, and Inclusion Antonio Farias sees Juneteenth as an opportunity to reexamine our nation's history. "Juneteenth is once again an opportunity for us as a nation to deepen our understanding of the horror embedded in our sanitized history. If we refuse to confront our past—the genocidal depopulation of Native American lands and subsequent repopulation with enslaved Africans—we will continue to tear at the fabric of our already fragile democracy," he said.

## Why Did It Take So Long for Texas to Free Slaves?

The Emancipation Proclamation extended freedom to enslaved people in Confederate States that were still under open rebellion. Making that order a reality depended on military victories by the U.S. Army and an ongoing presence to enforce them. It wasn't until more than two years later, in June of 1865, that U.S. Army troops arrived in Galveston Bay, Texas to officially announce and enforce emancipation.

Texas was the last state of the Confederacy in which enslaved people officially gained their freedom—a fact that is not well-known. "The observance is not widely known because Juneteenth is not celebrated in most of the U.S. and is only vaguely covered in history courses," Hearon said. "When I attended high school, the only courses offered were African American Literature and African American History. I never knew Juneteenth was considered a holiday because we were never given the day off in observance."

CU Chief Diversity Officer Theodosia S. Cook discussed why Juneteenth, and the knowledge of its history, matters. "Juneteenth symbolizes freedom, but it also acknowledges that the United States of America was built upon the denial of freedom for Black people," she said.

"In today's society, we see an immense denial of this history and the cruel irony that the Emancipation Proclamation was largely symbolic and not the end of chattel slavery in the U.S.," Cook said. "We know that laws in our country are being enacted to remove the facts of this history from our school systems. We know that brilliant scholars are being denied tenure because of their factual research. As a Black woman in America with ancestors who endured chattel slavery in Latin America, being married to a Black partner with ancestors from Mississippi who endured chattel slavery in the Deep South, who are now raising Black children in this nation, Juneteenth represents hope for a day when true freedom comes. I do truly look forward to a day of Freedom, Jubilee, and Liberation—when the history of our ancestors and this nation are embraced and not denied."

Juneteenth is particularly important because it comes after years of protests against police brutality. The Black Lives Matter movement may have shed light on the importance of Black history because in June 2021, a bill was proposed to make Juneteenth a federal holiday (one of the bill's authors was Vice President Kamala Harris). "Recently, there has been a renewed effort to make Juneteenth a national paid holiday," Hearon said. "It is important to not lose momentum or be distracted."

Racial injustice has continued in both direct and covert ways since the Union Army's proclamation finally forced Texas to free its enslaved people. Hearon pointed out that Black citizens continue to fight for equality, "I often wonder how far we've really advanced and what progress has been made, with the recent and continuous events of police brutality and structural racism against African Americans still occurring in our society," she said.

Acknowledging Juneteenth as a historical fact and teaching the event in schools is a start, but Hearon and the BFSA hope for more. "When will corporate leaders look different and policies be created in this country to protect us and our rights? Finally, when justice arrives, our voices will be heard, and we can be valued as people. Only then will we overcome and be free."

In Blackstone, 2021, the First Annual Juneteenth was formed and approved by Mayor William (Billy) Coleburn with his many appointed and volunteer committees.

The sign promoting the first Juneteenth Celebration read:

Juneteenth 26th-- Blackstone, Virginia
**Opening ceremonies are set for 9:30 a.m.**

In what promises to be a
big day, all systems are go for
**Blackstone's Juneteenth celebration**
this coming Saturday,

June 26th. Opening ceremonies
are set for 9:30 a.m.
in the Town Square.

# Honorees
of the Town's inaugural
Black History Heroes
will be announced at 1:00 p.m.

The overall event is set
for 10 a.m. to 10 p.m

78 vendors are expected.

# Come see and hear"The Speakers" At New Life Church 106 N. Main St Morning Session 10a-12n Afternoon Session 1p-3p

5/26/21, 6/4/21

Juneteenth Celebration Speaker Series

June 26th, 2021

Blackstone, VA

### African American History: Resilience, Enterprise, and Celebration

| 10AM: | 1PM: |
|---|---|
| Dr. Travis L.C. Warren, Pastor, Spring Hill Baptist Church, "The History of the Black Church" | Clarence Hawkes III, "Black History: Law and Politics" |
| 10:30AM: | 1:30PM: |
| Audrey L. Brown, President, NAACP Nottoway County Branch, "The History of the NAACP" | Dr. Edwina Wilson, "Health in the Black Community" |
| 11AM: | 2PM: |
| Chief Walter D. "Red Hawk" Brown, III Cheroenhaka (Nottoway) Indian Tribe, "Virginia Indian and African American History" | Charles Wilson, Realtor, Keller Williams Midlothian, "Buying a Home" |
| 11:30AM: | 2:30PM: |
| Cainan Townsend, Director of Education and Outreach, Robert Russa Moton Museum, "The History of the Moton School" | Nathaniel Miller, Council Member, Town of Blackstone, "Politics and Activism" |

# CHAPTER 3

# BLACKSTONE'S FIRST ANNUAL JUNETEENTH

## Honorees of the Town's Inaugural Black History Heroes

## Hometown Honorees

Blackstone Mayor Billy Coleburn presented 'Black History Heroes' plaques Saturday during the Town's Juneteenth Celebration. LEFT PHOTO: Shirley Austin Smith (accepting on behalf of honoree Rev. Dr. Frank Tucker); honoree Barbara Thompson; and Celeste Wynn, daughter of honoree the late Constance Wynn. RIGHT PHOTO: honoree Christine Davis Easterling, who offered brief remarks about her time at the former Luther Foster High School. As she has done since 2019, she continued her call for Nottoway officials to rename the old high school in Dr. Foster's memory.    *Photos by Tom Wilkinson, Isaiah Jones*

**Mayor William Coleburn Presented Black History Hero Award to Christine Davis Easterling**

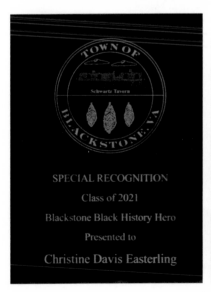

**Black History Hero Award Presented to Christine Davis Easterling**

# SORORITY SISTERS AND FRIENDS WHO ACCOMPANIED ME TO JUNETEENTH IN BLACKSTONE BY LIMOUSINE

Some members of the Alumni Association, sorority sisters and friends recommended Christine Easterling for the Black History Hero Award that was presented at the Juneteenth Celebration. Attorney Pamela Bethel, Awardee Christine Easterling, Soror Teola Jones and Deacon Emma Smith.

**AKA SORORS**
**FORMER RESIDENTS AND FRIENDS OF**
**BLACK HISTORY HEROES**

Shirley Smith, Emma Smith, Sallie Rich, Christine Easterling,
Kay Wallace

**Sharon Taylor Regina Charles, Lisa Christian, Janice Pace, Joy Marshall.**

Allen Lang, Webster Boose, Christine Easterling, Sharon Taylor,
Shirley Smith, Pamela Benson

**Mayor William Coleburn and Juneteenth visitors.**

**SHARON TAYLOR AND ATTORNEY PAMELA BENSON**

Photographer, Paul Jones of Silver Spring, Md.

Alvin Fowlkes and Mayor Billy

**MAYOR WILLIAM COLEBURN AND WIFE, JOYCE
ANZOLUT COLEBURN**

Sharon Taylor, Pamela Benson, Christine Easterling, Lisa Christian, Joy Marshall,

Sharon Taylor Live Streaming Juneteenth. Tommy Taylor, Melvin Austin, Shirley Smith, Mayor Billy Coleburn.

**CHRISTINE TALKING TO DEMOCRATIC CHAIRMAN THOMAS CREWS OF NOTTOWAY COUNTY DEMOCRATIC COMMITTEE**

**Melvin Austin Christine Easterling and Thomas Taylor**

**The Red Hatters with Queen Phillistine Epes**

# CHAPTER 4

# BLACKSTONE'S SECOND ANNUAL JUNETEENTH

## Three Days Away

Blackstone's second annual Juneteenth celebration is set for this coming Saturday, June 25th and has expanded. This year's festival will span three days with a vendor kick-off at 113 East Carolina Avenue in Crewe from 6:30 to 10 p.m. on Friday evening, June 24th. The next day (Saturday, June 25th) in downtown Blackstone, the festival will run from 10 a.m. to 10 p.m. On Sunday, June 26th, Burkeville's Juneteenth Committee will be hosting its first Combined Worship Service at 2:00 p.m. in the Nottoway High School Auditorium.

As this year's banner states -- but is partially blocked by Town's historical marker --Blackstone has set its Juneteenth celebrations for the last Saturday in June to avoid conflicting with other celebrations the prior week.

The Town of Blackstone last year and again this year provided the Juneteenth Committee $5,000 in operational funds. Blackstone's committee is being led again by Chastiddy Bryant, Ellen Eppes, and Erielle Eppes. For more information, call Ms. Bryant at 434-292-7251 ext. 227.

# BLACK HISTORY PANEL

## Honorees to be named at Juneteenth

A committee has been named at Town Hall to name the second class of honorees into Blackstone's "Black History Heroes" program.

Mayor Billy Coleburn recently appointed Council President Eric Nash, Councilwoman Annie Scott, Town Manager Philip Vannoorbeeck, and Director of Community Development Chastiddy Bryant.

Nominations were received during Black History Month, and honorees will be announced during the Town's second annual Juneteenth celebration on Saturday, June 25th. The Mayor will serve ex-officio.

The mayor said he would have included more members of Council, but three members would constitute a meeting under state open government laws.

Last year's honorees were **Christine Davis Easterling** of Silver Spring, Maryland, **Rev. Frank Tucker** of Laurel, Maryland, long-time Councilwoman **Barbara Thompson**, and the late councilwoman **Constance T. Wynn**.

# Black History Heroes, Class of 2022

## BLACKSTONE JUNETEENTH

## June 25, 2022

SECOND CLASS OF BLACK HISTORY HEROES,

WARREN JOHNSON, JR, JAMES CLARK, WILLIAM CLARK

MAYOR WILLIAM COLEBURN PRESENTING BLACK HISTORY
HERO AWARD TO MAJOR WARREN JOHNSON, JR.

**JOYCE COLEBURN AND MAYOR BILLY COLEBURN**

Christine Easterling and
Edward Thompson Jr.

Eunice and Christine Easterling

Rev. Colonel Hobbs and Wife Jean Hobbs

**LIVE MUSIC AT BLACKSTONE'S JUNETEENTH**

**Jeanette Johnson-Pouncy, Jacqueline Johnson, Warren Johnson Jr.,
Black History Honoree Class of 22, Christine Easterling**

CHRISTINE AND COMMITTEE MEMBER

SHARON STREAT

**Blackstone Juneteenth marks the day when, in 1865, enslaved people in Galveston, Texas, discovered they were finally free from being mere property.**

Mayor William Coleburn and his Wife Joyce Anzolut Coleburn

# Blackstone hosting second annual Juneteenth celebration

Photo by: Provided to WTVR

Town of Blackstone Juneteenth Celebration 2021

Honorees will be announced at the Town's 2nd annual Juneteenth celebration, which is set for Saturday, June 25th. Entries will be evaluated by a Town panel which is still being assembled.

Last year's honorees included the late **Constance T. Wynn**, who served on Council from 1987-2010; **Rev. Dr. Frank D. Tucker** of Laurel, Maryland, Senior Pastor of First Baptist Church in Washington, DC; and former NEA Teacher of the Year **Christine Davis Easterling** of Silver Spring, Maryland.

Also honored was former **Council President Barbara Thompson**, the longest-serving woman and longest-serving African-American to hold elected office in Nottoway County (March 1987-Sept. 2021).

# THE SECOND JUNETEENTH IN MY HOMETOWN

June 25, 2022

To The Town of Blackstone: The Honorable Mayor Coleburn and members of the Town Council.

I would like to thank you for honoring me with a "Special Recognition Award as part of the Blackstone Black History Hero Program.

My family roots were planted in the soil of Blackstone in 1829, when my great-great-grandfather migrated from Amelia County, Virginia. I was raised by a family tradition, to always treat people the way you want to be treated.

The window of my soul reflects Blackstone, and when you do things from your soul, you feel joy. During the festivities this past Saturday, I felt love in the air and joy beneath my feet, as I walked the streets of Blackstone. I am proud of my heritage and proud to call Blackstone, my hometown.

Again, many thanks to the leadership of the Town of Blackstone, my former teachers and classmates from Luther H. Foster High School, and family.

**Warren Johnson, Jr.**

**Class of 1962**

**Luther H. Foster High School**

**Jeanette Johnson-Pouncy and Christine Easterling, Author**

# CHAPTER 5
# MY BOOK—JUNETEENTH

I decided that I needed to write a book about Juneteenth in my hometown after the second celebration on June 25th, 2022. After this major celebration in my hometown, my major research about Juneteenth began to reach new altitudes. I was driven to continue to contribute to Juneteenth, participate in celebrations and further educate the world by writing a book about Juneteenth. In this book, I decided to discuss the efforts my hometown put forth to see that Juneteenth was taught, that people learned about and celebrated it.

It is important to write this book because too few people know about Juneteenth, and many had never heard about it or celebrated it.

The book came about when I discussed with the Mayor of Blackstone that I wanted to write the book and he said, "I am honored. I love it. It is so much more than a 'Black holiday It's as important as July 4th, which gave us the framework for June 1865. It should've happened much sooner. It's for ALL of us." The Town of Blackstone sign read in part: "THOSE WHO KNOW MUST TEACH." I am going to use my book to teach. My journey in writing the book is to do the research needed to teach and learn the real truth about Juneteenth. Further research described Juneteenth as a mashup of "June 19" which became a day of celebration for Black people in Texas, a tradition that slowly spread as they migrated to other states such as Louisiana and California. Even among Black people Texas declared Juneteenth a legal state holiday in 1980, the first state to do so, but national awareness has been spotty.

In June 1937, a ninety-two-year-old blind man named Felix Haywood explained it this way. This ninety-year-old formerly enslaved Texan named Felix Haywood talked to a WPA writer about the Civil War and its aftermath.

Felix reported: "Oh, we know what was goin' on in it all the time," said Haywood, "We had papers in them days just like now."

Heywood exposed a central canard of Juneteenth as a day when uninformed Blacks in Texas first learned they were free. In fact, General Gordon Granger and his 1,800 Union troops were not in Texas to deliver news to uninformed Blacks as much as they were there to enforce the law for recalcitrant whites. Juneteenth is built on falsehoods and wrapped in mistruths. The pillars of the day do not hold up to historical scrutiny.

It was also said by a writer named Stevenson, Brenda E. Stevenson, professor of history and African American studies at UCLA, whose most recent books include *What is Slavery*. She stated, "That no internet or telephones then, to spread the news, so when Union Major Gen. Gordon Granger arrived in Galveston, Texas—the most remote outpost of the Southern slave states—on June 19th, 1865, there were only unconfirmed rumors about the Emancipation Proclamation that had freed enslaved peoples more than two years earlier," Stevenson said.

Opal Lee, also known as the "Grandmother of Juneteenth," talked to ABC News.

"Juneteenth is not a Black thing and it's not a Texas thing," she told ABC News. "People all over, I don't care what nationality, we all bleed red blood. I was overjoyed. I was ecstatic," Lee told ABC News last year of her reaction to Juneteenth becoming a national holiday. "I was so happy I could have done a holy dance." A Texas native, Lee said she experienced racial unrest firsthand during her childhood, including a night, on June 19th, 1939, when a group of hundreds of rioters set fire to her family's home.

"The people didn't want us. They started gathering. The paper said the police couldn't control the mob. My father came with a gun and police told them if he busted a cap they'd let the mob have us," Lee told ABC station KTRK-TV in Houston. "They started throwing things at the house and when they left, they took out the furniture and burned it and burned the house. People have said that perhaps this is the catalyst that got me onto Juneteenth, I don't know that," she said. Juneteenth—also known as Freedom Day, Liberation Day and Emancipation Day—is celebrated on June 19th to mark the day in 1865 when African American slaves in Galveston, Texas, were among the last to be told they had been freed—a full two-and-a-half years after the Emancipation Proclamation outlawed slavery in the Confederacy and two months after the Civil War officially ended.

Opal Lee helped make Juneteenth a national holiday. At ninety-five, she's still had work to do. In 2016, then-eighty-nine-year-old Opal Lee walked from her home in Fort Worth, Texas, to the nation's capital in an effort to get Juneteenth named a national holiday. She attended the signing on Thursday.

When President Joe Biden signed a bill last year making Juneteenth a federal holiday commemorating the end of slavery in the United States, one woman captured well-deserved attention.

And Vice President Kamala Harris, the first Black vice president, also gave Lee her due in her remarks, saying, "And looking out across this room, I see the advocates, the activists, the leaders, who have been calling for this day for so long, including the one and only Ms. Opal Lee.

In 2016, at eighty-nine years old, Lee, a former teacher and lifelong activist, walked from her home in Fort Worth, Texas, to the nation's capital in an effort to get Juneteenth named a national holiday.

The celebration started with the freed enslaved people of Galveston, Texas. Although the Emancipation Proclamation freed enslaved people in the South in 1863, it could not be enforced in many places until after the end of the Civil War in 1865.

Laura Smalley, freed from a plantation near Bellville, Texas, remembered in a 1941 interview that her former master had gone to fight in the Civil War and came home without telling his slaves what had happened. "Old master didn't tell, you know, they was free," Smalley said at the time. "I think now they say they worked them, six months after that. Six months. And turn them loose on the 19th of June. That's why, you know, we celebrate that day."

Union Maj. Gen. Gordon Granger and his troops arrived at Galveston on June 19th, 1865, with news that the war had ended and that the enslaved were now free. That was more than two months after Confederate Gen. Robert E. Lee surrendered to Union Gen. Ulysses S. Grant in Virginia.

Granger delivered General Order No. 3, which said: "The people of Texas are informed that, in accordance with a proclamation from the Executive of the United States, all slaves are free. This involves an absolute equality of personal rights and rights of property between former masters and slaves, and the connection heretofore existing between them becomes that between employer and hired labor."

The next year, the now-free people started celebrating Juneteenth in Galveston. Its observance has continued around the nation and the world since. Events include concerts, parades and readings of the Emancipation Proclamation.

Juneteenth Museum Planned for Historic Fort Worth, Texas Neighborhood

## When did Juneteenth become a federal holiday?

**The Juneteenth National Independence Day Act was signed into law on June 17th, 2021, two days before the 2021 Juneteenth holiday.**

However, the vast majority of states already recognized Juneteenth as a holiday or a day of recognition, like Flag Day, and most states hold celebrations. For years, Juneteenth has been a paid holiday for state employees in Texas, New York, Virginia and Washington, and hundreds of companies give workers a day off for Juneteenth.

## When is Juneteenth 2022 and will federal employees get a day off?

This year, federal and private employers are giving workers the day off to observe the holiday on Monday, June 20th, because June 19th falls on a Sunday.

## Will markets and banks be closed for the holiday?

Yes, the Federal Reserve System and the New York Stock Exchange have added Juneteenth to their list of observed holidays and will be closed on Monday, June 20th, because June 19th falls on a Sunday.

Since most financial institutions follow the Fed's holiday schedule, the vast majority of banks are expected to be closed on Monday as well.

The U.S. Postal Service will also be closed on June 20th, as will all federal government buildings and government offices.

Historian writer Gregory P. Downs wrote, "Texas was a pariah state, where Southern whites dreamed of a white supremacist homeland. During the Civil War, white planters forcibly moved tens of thousands of slaves to Texas, hoping to keep them in bondage and away from the U.S. Army." Even after Lee's surrender at Appomattox, Texas governor Pendleton Murrah refused to surrender the state, fleeing to Mexico and leaving control of the state government, and the job of surrendering, to Confederate Lieutenant General Edmund Kirby.

He said, After Appomattox, white slaveholders in Texas kept Black men and women enslaved and killed them when they tried to assert their freedom. So, when Granger read General Order No. 3 to the public on Galveston Island, he was delivering a message not so much to enslaved men and women, but to their enslavers, and he was backing up that message with force.

"The people of Texas are informed that, in accordance with a proclamation from the Executive of the United States, all slaves are free," newspaper accounts reported Granger saying, emphasizing the word "all." Yet, even that statement was false.

# CHAPTER 6

# HOW JUNETEENTH BECAME A FEDERAL HOLIDAY

President Biden signed the Juneteenth National Independence Day Act into law Thursday, creating the first new federal holiday in nearly four decades. WSJ's Patrick Thomas explains how the signing could be a catalyst for more firms to observe the holiday. Photo: Evan Vucci/Associated Press.

(CNN) President Joe Biden said that signing legislation into law on Thursday establishing June 19th as Juneteenth National Independence Day—a US federal holiday commemorating the end of slavery in the United States—which will go down as "one of the greatest honors" of his presidency.

"I have to say to you, I've only been president for several months, but I think this will go down, for me, as one of the greatest honors I will have as president," Biden said at the White House during a signing ceremony.

"I regret that my grandchildren aren't here, because this is a really, really, really important moment in our history. By making Juneteenth a federal holiday, all Americans can feel the power of this day and learn from our history—and celebrate progress and grapple with the distance we've come (and) the distance we have to travel," Biden said.

The ceremony, which took place in the East Room, included some eighty members of Congress—including members of the Congressional Black Caucus, local elected officials, community leaders and activists. The President specifically noted that Opal Lee, the activist who campaigned to establish Juneteenth as a federal holiday, was in attendance.

Juneteenth commemorates June 19th, 1865, when Union Major General Gordon Granger announced the end of slavery in Galveston, Texas, in accordance with President Abraham Lincoln's 1863 Emancipation Proclamation. Only a handful of states currently observe Juneteenth as a paid holiday.

Biden, speaking at the White House alongside Vice President Kamala Harris, repeated the sentiments he relayed when he commemorated the Tulsa race massacre earlier this year, that "great nations don't ignore their most painful moments."

He said, "One year ago, I had the great honor of signing legislation to establish Juneteenth as a national holiday—the first new federal holiday since Dr. Martin Luther King, Jr. Day nearly four decades ago. Juneteenth marks both the long, hard night of slavery and subjugation and a promise of a brighter morning to come. It is a day of profound weight and power that reminds us of our extraordinary capacity to heal, hope, and emerge from our most painful moments into a better version of ourselves. Great nations don't ignore their most painful moments. They confront them to grow stronger. And that is what this great nation must continue to do.

"But it's not enough to just commemorate Juneteenth. Emancipation marked the beginning, not the end, of America's work to deliver on the promise of equality. To honor the true meaning of Juneteenth, we must not rest until we deliver the promise of America for all Americans.

"That is why Vice President Harris and I have appointed leadership in the federal government that looks like America. Our Administration is taking a whole-of-government approach to advance equity and racial justice and address the lasting impacts of systemic racism on Black communities. We have implemented initiatives to expand economic opportunity for Black families, provided historic support for Historically Black Colleges and Universities, improved health outcomes for Black communities, and taken important steps to protect voting rights, advance police reform, and enhance access to justice.

"This is a day to celebrate, to educate, and to act. As we mark Juneteenth, my Administration will continue our efforts to root out inequity from our country and institutions and ensure true liberty and justice for all."

Vice President Kamala Harris watched as Opal Lee (2nd L), the activist known as the grandmother of Juneteenth, was given a pen after President Joe Biden signed the Juneteenth bill.

Opal Lee Fought to Make Juneteenth a Federal Holiday. Opal Lee helped make Juneteenth a national holiday. At 95, she's still got work to do. Opal Lee, 95, helped make Juneteenth a national holiday. Now she wants to use it as an opportunity for education, healing and celebration.

This June 19th marks the second year the United States has observed Juneteenth as a national holiday. That's in large part due to the work and dedication of ninety-five-year-old Opal Lee, who played a major role in putting pressure on legislators to acknowledge a significant day Black folks in America have been celebrating for generations. National Independence Day Act, in the East Room of the White Jim Watson/AFP via Getty Images

Four years later, Lee's activism helped push Congress to establish a new national holiday for the first time in nearly forty years. In 1983, lawmakers designated Martin Luther King Jr. Day as the third Monday in January to memorialize the assassinated civil rights leader.

The national reckoning over race helped set the stage for Juneteenth to become the first new federal holiday since 1983 when Martin Luther King Jr. Day was created.

The bill was sponsored by Sen. Edward Markey, D-Mass., and had sixty co-sponsors. Bipartisan support emerged as lawmakers struggled to overcome divisions that are still simmering following the police killing last year of George Floyd in Minnesota.

Supporters of the holiday have worked to make sure Juneteenth celebrators don't forget why the day exists.

"In 1776 the country was freed from the British, but the people were not all free," Dee Evans, national director of communications of the National Juneteenth Observance Foundation, said in 2019. "June 19th, 1865, was actually when the people and the entire country was actually free."

There's also a sentiment to use the day to remember the sacrifices that were made for freedom in the United States, especially in these racially and politically charged days. Said Para LaNell Agboga, museum site coordinator at the George Washington Carver Museum, Cultural and Genealogy Center in Austin, Texas, "Our freedoms are fragile, and it doesn't take much for things to go backward."

2022 Last year, the U.S. government finally caught up with Black people who have been commemorating the end of slavery in the United States for generations with a day called "Juneteenth."

President Joe Biden established Juneteenth National Independence Day as a federal holiday when he signed into law a bill passed by both chambers of Congress.

The Senate approved the bill unanimously; only fourteen House Republicans—many representing states that were part of the slave-holding Confederacy in the 19th century—opposed the measure.

The Juneteenth National Independence Day Act was signed into law on June 17th, 2021, two days before the 2021 Juneteenth holiday.

However, the vast majority of states already recognized Juneteenth as a holiday or a day of recognition, like Flag Day, and most states hold celebrations. For years, Juneteenth has been a paid holiday for state employees in Texas, New York, Virginia and Washington, and hundreds of companies give workers a day off for Juneteenth.

## When is Juneteenth 2022 and will federal employees get a day off?

This year, federal and private employers are giving workers the day off to observe the holiday on Monday, June 20th, because June 19th falls on a Sunday. On Thursday, June 17th, 2021, President Joe Biden signed into law legislation making Juneteenth a federal holiday.

NASA Administrator Bill Nelson said in this year's Juneteenth Workforce Message, "Last year, President Biden signed legislation into law that established June 19th as Juneteenth National Independence Day—a federal holiday. On this day, we reckon with the moral stain of slavery on our country. We reflect on centuries of racial injustice, inequality, and struggle that unfortunately, still exist today.

"There is still more work to do, and it is work we must all do. I encourage all members of the NASA family to participate in a Juneteenth celebration and reflect on this historic event in our history. Let us reaffirm and rededicate ourselves to building a more perfect union."

This image of Galveston and Bolivar Peninsula, separated by the Galveston Bay, were taken by the crew of the International Space Station as it orbited 262 miles above. In the image, Galveston Island is at right, Bolivar Peninsula at left, with the top of the picture being southeast.

Premiering on Juneteenth, Sunday, June 19th, *The Color of Space* is a fifty-minute inspirational documentary by NASA that tells the stories of Black Americans determined to reach the stars. It will be available to watch starting at noon EDT on NASA TV, the NASA app, NASA social media channels, and the agency's website.

# CHAPTER 7

# WHAT DO THE JUNETEENTH COLORS AND SYMBOLS REPRESENT?

A Juneteenth flag was created in 1997 that included the
colors red, white and blue.

Many Black people celebrate Juneteenth with a
flag that is red, black and green.

The first flag representing Juneteenth was created in 1997 by Ben
Haith, the founder of the National Juneteenth Celebration Foundation
(NJCF). Artist Lisa Jeanne Graf stated on her site she "fine-tuned" the
version of the original contributors, also including Verlene Hines, Azim
and Eliot Design, resulting in the flag waved with pride at Juneteenth
marches today. Set in a blue and red horizontally banded background, a
white star sits in the center, surrounded by another twelve-pointed star.
The National Juneteenth Observance Foundation claims flag designer
Haith led the holiday's initial flag-raising ceremony in Boston's Roxbury
Heritage Park.

People carry a Juneteenth flag as they march during a Juneteenth re-enactment celebration in Galveston, Texas, on June 19th, 2021. The first flag representing Juneteenth was created in 1997 by Ben Haith. Haith told CNN last year, "This country has so many aspects to it that are spiritual, and I believe this flag is of that nature. It [the idea for the design] just came through me."

According to NJOF, all the individual symbols depicted in the Juneteenth flag have been carefully designed to represent specific themes important to the movement.

**The Arc:** The flag's horizontal aspect is an attempt to symbolize both fresh opportunities and promising futures for Black Americans.

**The Star:** This refers to both The Lone Star State of Texas, where Juneteenth was first celebrated, and the freedom of every Black American across the nation.

**The Star's Outline:** The other white mark outlining the star's perimeter is thought to reflect a nova, representing a new and optimistic rebirth for the nation.

An American flag is reflected off Anastacia McClesky's sunglasses during Broadway Celebrates Juneteenth in Times Square on June 19, 2021, in New York City. The Juneteenth flag uses the same colors as the U.S. flag, red, white, and blue. Experts at the language learning platform Babbel note Juneteenth is being marked in many ways this year. They told Newsweek, "There are many ways to commemorate Juneteenth, centered around supporting, celebrating and learning about Black history, culture, and life. In the United States, there will be several formal events, street fairs, parades and concerts occurring in honor of the holiday. Globally, you can celebrate Juneteenth by supporting Black-owned businesses: from restaurants and cafés to small businesses, artists, authors, poets, and leaders within the Black community, supporting and supporting up for Black communities during the holiday is just one way to celebrate black culture year-round."

The Babbel experts also note how self-education is another important tool to tap into Juneteenth, and beyond.

There's a richness and exuberance in the **color red** that resonated for those who first celebrated Juneteenth. Interestingly enough, there is also a more diaspora-driven reason why the color red is so important to Juneteenth dishes.

"Texas was at the end of the world to the Antebellum South. There were a lot of enslaved Africans who were coming to Texas from the continent and through the Caribbean. The color red is highly associated with the cultures that would've come through the later years of the trade, which would have been Yoruba and Kongo," culinary historian and writer Michael Twitty shared with *Oprah Daily*. And as Chef Millie Peartree wrote, the color red also "symbolizes and is the representation of the bloodshed and resilience of enslaved people."

From specialty drinks to main courses, there is certainly no shortage of red foods at a proper Juneteenth celebration. The most popular red foods are Juneteenth Punch, red velvet cupcakes, and hot links.

## What Is a Prosperity Meal and Why Is It Served?

Many of us are likely familiar with the intoxicating aroma of a pot of black-eyed peas cooking on New Year's Eve. And on the burner next to it? A simmering pot of collard greens. These foods are prepared on December 31st to ring in the new year and bring good fortune.

Six months later, on Juneteenth, those two dishes and others are summoned once again for a similar purpose. Prosperity meals on Juneteenth are "all about celebrating good luck and wishing for the best," said Michiel Perry, lifestyle expert and creator of the brand Black Southern Belle. The meals often include side dishes like black-eyed peas, collard greens, cornbread, cabbage, and sweet potatoes.

## What Are the Most Popular Juneteenth Dishes?

Whether you're a Patti in the kitchen or more of a beginner, there's a variety of Juneteenth-inspired recipes you can whip up for the holiday. They range in difficulty from simple to "just leave that dish to your auntie."

Cornbread is always a great place to start, and it's a must on Juneteenth. It's simple enough for just about anyone to make, and even kids can get in on this one. To make cornbread, combine bacon fat (or canola oil), cornmeal, baking soda, kosher salt, honey, egg, buttermilk, and butter. Bake and you're all set!

If you really want to chef it up on Juneteenth, fried catfish is the way to go. Dredging and frying are a must, and adding your own special seasonings is always welcome.

Feeling thirsty? You can't go wrong with a cold glass of Juneteenth Punch. This ruby red drink combines cranberry juice, ginger ale (or 7Up), strawberry sorbet, and a handful of fruit juices. It's particularly refreshing in the sweltering June heat.

No matter how you celebrate Juneteenth this year, paying homage to those who came before us, showing respect, and enjoying good eats are all necessary ingredients.

They said: "Reading educational materials and engaging in socio-political rhetoric from Black perspectives can make a positive impact on society's awareness of, and ability to identify and take action against systemic racism. Documentaries, books, podcasts, and even social media pages made by Black creators are great and accessible sources of these types of materials.

You can also take a more politically direct route to show support for the Black community: donating your time or money to reputable organizations such as the NAACP [The National Association for the Advancement of Colored People] or NBJC [National Black Justice Coalition], supporting local and national Black charities, and signing petitions in support of Black freedom and rights are all excellent ways to show up for this community, on Juneteenth and beyond."

There's a richness and exuberance in the **color red** that resonated for those who first celebrated Juneteenth. Interestingly enough, there is also a more diaspora-driven reason why the color red is so important to Juneteenth dishes.

"Texas was at the end of the world to the Antebellum South. There were a lot of enslaved Africans who were coming to Texas from the continent and through the Caribbean. The color red is highly associated with the cultures that would've come through the later years of the trade, which would have been Yoruba and Kongo," culinary historian and writer Michael Twitty shared with *Oprah Daily*.

And as Chef Millie Peartree wrote, the color red also "symbolizes and is the representation of the bloodshed and resilience of enslaved people."

From specialty drinks to main courses, there is certainly no shortage of red foods at a proper Juneteenth celebration. The most popular red foods are Juneteenth Punch, red velvet cupcakes, and hot links.

# ABOUT THE AUTHOR

Dean Christine Davis Easterling is a retired teacher and school administrator who served students in Washington, DC, for over thirty years. As a certified dean of Standard Leadership Schools in affiliation with the National Baptist Convention, USA, she's responsible for accrediting church schools. She's also the past president of the District of Columbia Retired Educators Association.

Christine Easterling displays her certification as dean of Christian education at First Baptist Church in Northwest Washington, DC. She is an active member of First Baptist Church in Northwest Washington. At First Baptist, she's served as a member of the Board of Christian Education, director of Vacation Bible School, and chairperson of the fall and spring institutes. She's been a member of the First Baptist Gospel Choir for fifteen years. She is a retired teacher and school administrator who worked for more than thirty years in the District of Columbia public school system. She is the former president of the DC Retired Educators Association (DCREA) and author of *Inspirational Treasures: Essays by Educators and the Students Reflecting the Joy of Teaching*. She also wrote *A Giant for Justice: Biography of William H. "Bill" Simons*, which is a twenty-five-year history of the Washington teachers union. She teaches a "Miracles of Jesus" class for the Baptist Congress of Christian Education, state of Maryland, from her latest book, titled *The Miracles of Jesus*. She has been cited on numerous occasions for her outstanding work in the local education arena and in the DC community. She was recently certified as dean of Standard Leadership Training Schools in affiliation with the National Baptist Convention, USA Inc., receiving her certification at the annual northeast regional conference. She performs community service with a global perspective as a fifty-year member of Alpha Kappa Alpha Sorority, Inc.

# PRIMARY SOURCES

ABC station KTRK-TV in Houston

President Biden signed the Juneteenth National Independence Day Act into law.

Stevenson, Brenda E. Stevenson, professor of history and African American studies at UCLA

Congressional Black Caucus

Chef Millie Peartree

Getty Images

Ben Haith MARK FELIX/GETTY IMAGES

Haith told CNN

Caroline Coleburn, WTVR Chanel 6 News

Richmond, Virginia

*Posted at 11:00 AM, Jun 21, 2022*

*Blackstone, Virginia Juneteenth Committee*

Chastiddy Bryant, Director of Community Development

The Juneteenth National Independence Day Act

William Coleburn, Mayor of Blackstone, Virginia

Black History Heroes

The Babbel experts

Blackstone History Committee and sub-committee.

Bragg, Ko. "The Historical Legacy of Juneteenth."

"National Museum of African American History and Culture, 18 June 2020, nmaahc.si.edu/blog-post/historical-legacy-Juneteenth.

"The Long History of Juneteenth, and Why the Fight Is Not Over Yet." News Northeastern The Long History of Juneteenth and Why the Fight Is Not over – Yet Comments – 18 June 2020,news.northeastern.edu/2020/06/18/ the-long-history-of-juneteenth-and-why-the-fights-not-over-yet/.

On June 19th, 1865, the last of the enslaved people in Galveston, Texas were told by Union soldiers that they were free, two years following the signing of the Emancipation Proclamation by Abraham Lincoln. On June 17th, 2021, President Biden signed the bill into law, making Juneteenth the 11th holiday recognized by the federal government. On this day our communities come together to celebrate African American cultural heritage and the symbolic day of freedom for the Black community.

African American Experience database free to use with your Allegheny County library card. Don't have a library card? Sign up for one online for free here. If you enjoy this book list and would like to get more recommendations tailored to your interests, fill out our Book Recommendation form and a librarian will curate a list for you!

Michael Twitty shared with *Oprah Daily*.

*Mayor William Billy Coleburn is the retired mayor of Blackstone, Virginia. He is also the publisher of the Blackstone Courier Newspaper*